BRIGHT IDEA BOOKS

JASON
Reynolds

by Golriz Golkar

CAPSTONE PRESS
a capstone imprint

Bright Idea Books are published by Capstone Press
1710 Roe Crest Drive, North Mankato, Minnesota 56003
www.mycapstone.com

Library of Congress Cataloging-in-Publication Data
Names: Golkar, Golriz, author.
Title: Jason Reynolds / by Golriz Golkar.
Description: North Mankato, Minnesota : Bright Idea Books, [2019] | Series:
  Influential people | Includes bibliographical references and index.
Identifiers: LCCN 2018019500 (print) | LCCN 2018025446 (ebook) | ISBN
  9781543541717 (ebook) | ISBN 9781543541311 (hardcover : alk. paper)
Subjects: LCSH: Reynolds, Jason--Juvenile literature. | African American
  authors--21st century--Biography--Juvenile literature. | Children's
  stories--Authorship--Juvenile literature.
Classification: LCC PS3618.E9753 (ebook) | LCC PS3618.E9753 Z68 2019 (print)
  | DDC 813/.6 [B] --dc23
LC record available at https://lccn.loc.gov/2018019500

Editorial Credits
Editor: Mirella Miller
Designer: Becky Daum
Production Specialist: Ryan Gale

Quote Sources
p. 4, "Meet the Author: Jason Reynolds." *Youtube*, October 4, 2017; p. 5, "Meet the Author: Jason
Reynolds." *Youtube*, October 4, 2017

Photo Credits
AP Images: Paul Morigi, 6–7, Rolf Vennenbernd/picture-alliance/dpa, cover, 8–9; Getty Images: Bill
O'Leary/The Washington Post, 20–21, 25, Marvin Joseph/The Washington Post, 22, Mireya Acierto/
FilmMagic, 12, 28; iStockphoto: fstop123, 30–31; Newscom: Beowulf Sheehan/ZUMA Press, 18,
Rolf Vennenbernd/dpa/picture-alliance, 26; Rex Features: M. Stan Reaves, 17, MediaPunch, 5;
Shutterstock Images: Kathy Hutchins, 15, Orhan Cam, 11

Design Elements: iStockphoto, Red Line Editorial, and Shutterstock Image

TABLE OF CONTENTS

CHAPTER 1

A CELEBRITY
Author

Jason Reynolds was on a library visit. He was giving advice to teenagers. He told them why it is important to read. "Read and write. . . . It breaks down barriers."

The students listened carefully. They asked him many questions. They were excited to meet their favorite author. Reynolds loved getting kids to read. He finished with a nice message. "I love you. . . . You all don't have to know people to love them."

Reynolds speaks at many events every year.

Reynolds posed with one of his books at a bookstore in New York.

CONNECTING WITH READERS

Reynolds knows how to talk to teenagers. He writes young adult **fiction**. His characters seem similar to real people. They have problems that are important to readers. They go on adventures. The characters have dreams and hopes. Reynolds wants young people to connect with his books.

Reynolds did not enjoy reading when he was young. He stopped reading at age 9. Years passed before he read a book for fun again. Who would have believed Reynolds would become a famous author one day?

Now people enjoy the books Reynolds writes. His books are **best sellers**. They have won many awards.

MANY BOOKS

Reynolds has published 10 books in four years.

Reynolds wasn't sure he'd become an author later in life.

9

CHAPTER 2

A BOY WHO DID Not Like to Read

Jason Reynolds was born in Washington, D.C. He was not a strong student. His teachers thought he needed to try harder. Reynolds' mom was a teacher. She told him he could do anything. He just needed to believe in himself.

Reynolds' education started in Washington, D.C.

Reynolds talked about his work on a book tour.

Reynolds did not enjoy the books
he read. The characters were not like
him. They were not African Americans.
Reynolds' neighborhood had problems.
There were drugs. There was violence.
Reynolds never read about those issues.
He wanted to read about experiences he
could connect with.

A MUSICAL CONNECTION

Reynolds bought a rap music album when he was 9 years old. It was made by Queen Latifah. He loved it. The words sounded similar to the way he talked. The songs told stories he understood. The **lyrics** were like poems. Reynolds saw words in a new way.

FINISHING A NOVEL

Reynolds finished reading his first novel, *Black Boy*, at age 17. The characters reminded Reynolds of his friends and himself.

Reynolds looks up to rapper Queen Latifah.

CHAPTER 3

PICKING UP
the Pen

Reynolds began writing poetry every day at age 9. He wrote the way he talked. Rap and hip-hop music inspired him.

Reynolds studied English in college. He continued writing poems. He also worked at a bookstore. They sold books written by African Americans. He found books by authors he did not know before. He was finally reading again!

Reynolds enjoys discussing his books with his fans.

"DO NOT FEAR WHAT HAS BEEN BLOWN UP IF YOU MUST FEAR THE UNEXPLODED"

Poets such as Suheir Hammad inspired Reynolds to keep writing.

18

—SUHEIR HAMMAD

Reynolds decided to publish a book of poems in 2009. It was unsuccessful. Reynolds was sad. He had no money left. He had finished college. But his grades had been low. Graduate schools rejected him. Reynolds took many different jobs. He wanted to quit writing for good.

KEEP TRYING

Reynolds once failed an English class. But he never gave up. He kept on writing.

Then his old childhood friend stepped in. Christopher Myers is a famous author. So was Myers' dad. Myers told Reynolds to keep writing. He told Reynolds someone needs to write about **urban** kids. Reynolds understands them well. These kids rarely read about their lives in books. They need someone to tell their stories. Reynolds listened to his friend.

Reynolds talked about his book, *Ghost*.

As Brave As You is one of Reynolds's fiction titles.

FINDING SUCCESS

Reynolds wrote his first novel, *When I Was the Greatest,* in 2014. It was **controversial** for some people. It mentioned drugs and guns. Most people loved it. It felt like a real story. It was a big success. Reynolds won his first book award. He realized he loved writing fiction. He wrote other books such as *As Brave As You.* This book also won an award.

CHAPTER 4

HELPING OTHERS
Find Their Voices

Reynolds has published many books. He is a **prolific** writer. He writes every day. Reynolds wants to make his writing better. He even teaches writing at a university.

Reynolds loves talking to young people. He visits schools and community centers. He makes more than 100 visits every year. He talks about the power of books. He tells people how books can help us.

Reynolds has many ideas for future books.

Reynolds is a positive influence for young readers.

Reynolds also visits **juvenile detention centers**. He helps the kids there. He tells them to resist violence. He tells them to choose a better life.

Reynolds is a true inspiration. He makes young people want to read and write. They understand his books. His stories relate to their lives.

NEW NOVELS

Reynolds published two novels in 2018, *Sunny* and *For Every One*.

GLOSSARY

best seller
a top-selling book

controversial
involving a long public debate
with different opinions

fiction
books that describe imaginary
events and people

juvenile detention center
a prison for young people,
usually under age 18

lyrics
the words in a song

prolific
producing many works

urban
having to do with cities

TIMELINE

1983: Jason Reynolds is born in Washington, D.C.

1991: He buys Queen Latifah's rap album *Black Reign*, which makes him interested in poetry.

2005: He graduates from the University of Maryland with a B.A. degree in English.

2009: He publishes his book, *My Name Is Jason. Mine Too.: Our Story. Our Way* with his artist friend Jason Griffin.

2014: He publishes his first successful book, *When I Was the Greatest.*

2016: He publishes *Ghost*, the first book in his best-selling Track series.

2016: He wins the important Kirkus Prize for his novel *As Brave As You*.

ACTIVITY

WRITE A POEM

Before he wrote novels, Jason Reynolds wrote poetry as a child. He wrote about the things he and other kids from his neighborhood experienced in their daily lives. Think about something interesting from your life. Is there a special activity you and your friends like? Is there a place you like to visit? Can you describe the people who live in your neighborhood? Write a poem in any style you like—rhyming or not—about life in your neighborhood.

FURTHER RESOURCES

Interested in learning more about Jason Reynolds? Learn more here:

Jason Reynolds's Website
http://www.jasonwritesbooks.com

Jason Reynolds Is the Hardest-Working Man in Washington
https://www.publishersweekly.com/pw/by-topic/childrens/childrens-authors/
article/74244-jason-reynolds-is-the-hardest-working-man-in
-washington.html

Learn more about what Jason Reynolds has to say here:

Jason Reynolds Says That All Kids Like to Read
http://kpcnotebook.scholastic.com/post/jason-reynolds-says-all-kids-read

Interview with Author Jason Reynolds
https://superiorspidertalk.com/ultimate-spin-62-interview-w-miles-morales
-author-jason-reynolds-podcast/

INDEX